P9-DHE-684

Rain, Rain, Rain Forest

Rain, Rain,

BRENDA Z. GUIBERSON

Illustrated by
STEVE JENKINS

Rain Forest

Henry Holt and Company

New York

*S*plitter, *splat, splash!* Rain gushes into
the rain forest. It soaks the moss, drizzles off
dangling vines, and thrums against slick waxy
leaves that serve as umbrellas for dozens of small
creatures. Twenty feet of rain can fall in a year, and
most of the time the forest is squishy like a swamp.
In this deluge, every crevice and cup high in the
trees overflows with water.

Keeecheeew! A dangling sloth sneezes slowly. He has
been asleep for sixteen hours but now stirs awake in
the pounding rain. He is so wet that green algae
grow in his fur. Moths live in the fur and eat the
algae. Hundreds of ticks, fleas, and beetles live there
too. The sloth eats leaves. He chews and digests
VERY slowly. Now protected from hungry jaguars by
the thrum and splatter of the water, the sloth begins
a slow journey to the forest floor. Moving at just six
feet a minute, he passes a bathing macaw as the rain
trickles to a stop.

Aroo-hoo-hoo. High above the sloth, howler
monkeys roar in a noisy chorus and sip water
that drips from the leaves. Near them a plant
called a tank bromeliad is flooded with almost
a gallon of water.

A salamander lives between the moist
leaves, where its porous skin will not dry out.
A mosquito buzzes in to lay eggs in the water.
Then a tiny poison-dart frog sees the pools in the
bromeliad. *Hop, hop, hop!* The water signals her to
start a journey too. She follows the sloth down
to the forest floor.

At the base of the tree the sloth digs a hole with his stubby tail. Moths and beetles fly out of his fur and lay eggs in the droppings he leaves behind. When the larvae hatch in the droppings they will have plenty to eat. As the sloth climbs back up, the rainwater turns to hot, muggy steam.

Kwak, crrrik, crrrik! Keel-billed toucans glide through the mist, looking for a dry hole in a tree. Finally they find a cavity big enough to raise a chick. The forest has a housing shortage, and green parrots arrive to squabble over the space. *Kwak!* The toucans swing long rainbow beaks up, down, and all around to keep the nest for themselves.

Back on the forest floor the poison-dart frog hops
over to the tadpoles she left there. Not much rain
trickles this far down through the trees, but the little
tadpoles have kept moist in a pile of wet leaves. The
frog waits for one of them to wiggle onto her back.
Then she carries it up the tree, past the dangling
sloth, to the tank bromeliad. *Splish*. The shiny
tadpole slips into a pool in the plant, and
the frog lays two extra eggs for it to eat.
A tarantula watches the frog but stays
away. Bright colors warn that this
frog oozes poison.

The sloth is exhausted from his weekly bathroom journey. By sunset, he has already been asleep for hours. To save energy his body temperature drops to the coolness of the night air. Nearby a capuchin monkey and her baby sip rainwater, then curl up on a bed of moss. While they sleep, the forest fills with the sounds of the night creatures. *Sloop!* A silky anteater slurps up thousands of ants. *Flap flap!* A fruit bat bites a fig. *Hssss.* An emerald tree boa thrusts its tongue to taste the air. The air carries the taste of mouse. Everywhere night creatures with huge bright eyes slither and slurp through the darkness.

In the morning
the sloth moves to the
wide open branches of a
cecropia tree to bask in the
sunlight. The little capuchin tries
to follow, but angry azteca ants boil
out of holes in the cecropia trunk. They attack with strong
biting jaws and sprays of acid. The monkey quickly swings
back to its mother.

The ants raise aphids in the hollow parts of the tree.
The aphids turn tree juices into a sugary honeydew that
the ants eat. The ants keep all intruders away from the
tree—except the sloth. The sloth
hardly notices the ant
attack with all the
moths, ticks, and
beetles living in
his thick fur.

The poison-dart frog looks for other bromeliads for the rest of her tadpoles. There are none in the cecropia, but the tree next to it has twenty different kinds. There are also dozens of types of ants. The leafcutters use scissorlike jaws to slice up the leaves. In a wobbly line, they haul the heavy green chunks back to their underground nest.

At the nest the smallest leafcutters chop and chew the leaves to grow a fungus garden. The colony has four million ants, all hungry for fungus. *Snip, carry, chop, chew.* As the gardeners trim away leaves from the rain forest, more light shines in and more rain drizzles down to help the low plants grow.

There is no rain in the rain forest for a few days.
Some of the trees start to drop their leaves. The sloth
moves to a branch with more shadows.
The poison-dart frog deposits more eggs
for her tadpoles and then tucks her
long limbs under her body to keep them
moist. The bromeliad's pools are filling with
leaves, drowned insects, droppings, and dust.
Special pores in the bromeliad absorb this rotting
debris to use for food. With little water to drink, the
capuchins eat juicy ripe fruit. *Plop!* A mango drops
to the forest floor, and a white-tailed deer comes
close for a nibble. Then a blue morpho butterfly
flutters in for a sip of juice.

Brawk! Brawk! Suddenly
the capuchins cry out in
alarm. A harpy eagle is flying
overhead. *Snap, crash!* The
monkeys flee, but the slow
sloth does not blink or twitch.
In the shadows he looks like
a tree branch and the eagle
does not see him. Instead
the huge bird with five-inch
talons swoops after a
monkey to carry
home for
her chick.

On a low branch the capuchins gather with squeals
and shrieks. They comfort one another by grooming, or
plucking insects from one another's fur. They sip water
from a tree hole until nothing is left. Near them
a six-foot-long iguana nibbles an orchid leaf.
Without rain the orchid will not bloom,
but it has swollen "bulbs" where it stores
enough water to survive. *Drip, drip, drip!*
A misty rain begins. The orchid absorbs
some of this moisture through its
dangling roots, but there is not nearly
enough to swamp the treetops.

People come into the forest. Below the dangling sloth a man from a nearby village shows a scientist the orange-colored blossoms he uses to treat snakebites. Then he points to the capuchins rubbing against a plant that makes a chemical that keeps insects away. Suddenly a beetle with a curved green horn drops from the sloth onto the arm of the scientist. The scientist is excited. It is one she has never seen before. Almost every day she discovers something new in the rain forest.

Zing. The scientist
shoots a line into the tree and
climbs up into the canopy of leaves.
In the bromeliads she looks for a frog that produces
a strong chemical able to reduce pain. From this she
is hoping to make a new medicine. Then she collects
the leaves the capuchins rubbed against their fur.
The monkeys have led her to a plant that might keep
pests away from people and crops. She comes down
quickly as a dark cloud blows in.

CRACK! SNAZZ! Lightning flashes. Rain, rain, rain pours into the rain forest. *Splosh-splat! Thrum thrum thrum.* The torrent refills the tanks of the bromeliads, splashes the sloth, trickles down the tangle of trees and vines, and seeps into the scientist's boots. *Splitter, splat, thrum.* The forest overflows with nourishing drops. Soon new leaves and blossoms, seeds and fruit will pop out everywhere. And the water will drizzle down clean and clear for all the creatures to drink.

For all the rain forest creatures,
past and present, named and unnamed
—B. Z. G.

For Jamie
—S. J.

Many thanks to Laura Godwin, Reka Simonsen, Martha Rago,
and the others at Holt who helped with this book

Henry Holt and Company, LLC
Publishers since 1866
115 West 18th Street
New York, New York 10011
www.henryholt.com

Library of Congress Cataloging-in-Publication Data
Guiberson, Brenda Z.
Rain, rain, rain forest / Brenda Z. Guiberson; illustrated by Steve Jenkins.
Summary: Takes a journey through a rain forest, investigating the plants and animals that dwell there.
1. Rain forest ecology—Juvenile literature. 2. Rain forest animals—Juvenile literature. 3. Rain forest plants—Juvenile literature.
[1. Rain forests. 2. Rain forest ecology. 3. Rain forest animals. 4. Rain forest plants. 5. Ecology.]   I. Jenkins, Steve, ill.   II. Title.
QH541.5.R27G85 2004   577.34—dc22   2003012250

ISBN 0-8050-6582-2 / First Edition—2004 / Designed by Martha Rago and Patrick Collins
The artist used cut-paper collage to create the illustrations for this book.
Printed in the United States of America on acid-free paper. ∞

1   3   5   7   9   10   8   6   4   2